P

Knowing the value of something and the
esteem we should have for it. Knowing what a
particular item can be used for educates us and
propels us to use it in ways we might not have
thought of apart from the information we might
be given.

God's Word. The Word of God. The Statutes of
God. The Law. God's Precepts. God's
Judgments. The Bible. These are all different
names for the same thing – the written words that
God has directed to be written and preserved in
one book.

We will be gaining an appreciation of the Word of
God and instructions on what He has given it to
us for. We will be learning of our interaction with
it and many promises associated with the proper
esteem of, use of and response to the Word of
God.

Here is a wonderful assessment as found one of the
Gideon's International Ministries' opening pages
of their widely distributed New Testament and
Psalms pocket bibles:

*"THE BIBLE contains the mind of God, the state of
man, the way of salvation, the doom of sinners,
and the happiness of believers. Its doctrines are
holy, its precepts are binding, its histories are true,
and its decisions are immutable. Read it to be
wise, believe it to be safe, and practice it to be*

1

holy. It contains light to direct you, food to support you, and comfort to cheer you.

"It is the traveler's map, the pilgrim's staff, the pilot's compass, the soldier's sword, and the Christian's charter. Here Paradise is restored, Heaven opened, and the gates of hell disclosed.

"CHRIST is its grand subject, our good the design, and the glory of God its end.

"It should fill the memory, rule the heart, and guide the feet. Read it slowly, frequently and prayerfully. It is a mine of wealth, a paradise of glory, and a river of pleasure. It is given you in life, will be opened at the judgment, and be remembered forever. It involves the highest responsibility, will reward the greatest labor, and will condemn all who trifle with its sacred contents."

I hope and pray that this delve into Psalm 119 will reignite our passion for His Word, cultivate a greater desire to know its contents and draw us closer to the Author than ever before.

In Christ,

Maureen Schaffer

Special thanks to A.J. Hulsey for contributing questions for week four.

Psalm 119

Introduction

Ps 119:1-8

1 Blessed are the undefiled in the way,

Who walk in the law of the Lord!

2 Blessed are those who keep His testimonies,

Who seek Him with the whole heart!

3 They also do no iniquity;

They walk in His ways.

4 You have commanded us

To keep Your precepts diligently.

5 Oh, that my ways were directed

To keep Your statutes!

6 Then I would not be ashamed,

When I look into all Your commandments.

7 I will praise You with uprightness of heart,

When I learn Your righteous judgments.

8 I will keep Your statutes;

Oh, do not forsake me utterly!

1. List some names used in Psalm 119 for the Word of God:_____

_____

_____

_____

_____

_____

_____

2. Describe your relationship with the bible BEFORE you gave your life to Christ or, if you have not surrendered to Christ what do you think of this book?_____

_____

_____

_____

_____

_____

_____

_____

3. What is your current relationship with God's Word? Use, attitude, version you are using, what you are studying.....etc._____

_____

_____

_____

_____

_____

_____

4. Look at the following verses. Underline those words that stand out to you and jot down any thoughts about them.

John 17:17-18 - "Sanctify them by Your truth. Your word is truth." _____

_____

_____

_____

_____

Ps 138:2b - "For You have magnified Your word above all Your name." _____

_____

_____

_____

_____

Eph 6:17 - "And take the helmet of salvation, and the sword of the Spirit, which is the word of God;" _____

_____

_____

_____

_____

_____

_____

_____

_____

1 Peter 1:24-25 - "All flesh is as grass, And all the glory of man as the flower of the grass. The grass withers, And its flower falls away, But the word of the Lord endures forever." _____

_____

_____

_____

_____

_____

_____

_____

Isa 55:10-11 - "For as the rain comes down, and the snow from heaven, And do not return there, But water the earth, And make it bring forth and bud, That it may give seed to the sower And bread to the eater, So shall My word be that goes forth from My mouth; It shall not return to Me void, But it shall accomplish what I please, And it shall prosper in the thing for which I sent it.

_____

_____

_____

_____

_____

_____

_____

_____

Ps 1:1-3 - Blessed is the man Who walks not in the counsel of the ungodly, Nor stands in the path of sinners, Nor sits in the seat of the scornful; But his delight is in the law of the Lord, And in His law he meditates day and night. He shall be like a tree Planted by the rivers of water, That brings forth its fruit in its season, Whose leaf also shall not wither; And whatever he does shall prosper. _____

_____

_____

_____

_____

_____

_____

_____

_____

_____

_____

_____

Whole Heart

Ps 119:9-16

9 How can a young man cleanse his way?

By taking heed according to Your word.

10 With my whole heart I have sought You;

Oh, let me not wander from Your commandments!

11 Your word I have hidden in my heart,

That I might not sin against You.

12 Blessed are You, O Lord!

Teach me Your statutes.

13 With my lips I have declared

All the judgments of Your mouth.

14 I have rejoiced in the way of Your testimonies,

As much as in all riches.

15 I will meditate on Your precepts,

And contemplate Your ways.

16 I will delight myself in Your statutes;

I will not forget Your word.

1. We all need our paths cleansed. What does
   Psalm 119:9 say can cleanse our paths?_____

   _____

   _____

   _____

   _____

2. Why do you think the Lord particularly mentions
   the YOUNG man in verse 9?_____

   _____

   _____

   _____

3. Describe some disciplines of a believer who is
   actively seeking God with their whole heart?_____

   _____

   _____

   _____

   _____

   _____

4. What would be some symptoms that we might
   be 'wandering' from His commandments?_____

   _____

   _____

   _____

   _____

   _____

5. Where does verse 11 say we are to hide His
   Word?_____

   _____

6. What does Proverbs 2:1-5 say about hiding God's Word within us and what will it result in?_____

_____
_____
_____
_____
_____
_____
_____
_____

7. What does verse 11 say that hiding God's Word in our hearts will result in?_____

_____

8. So what place does the Word of God have in our fight against sin?_____

_____

9. Looking at verse 12, who is the One who can cause us to understand the words?_____

_____

10. What is the psalmist doing in order to assure the 'teacher' will teach him?_____

_____
_____

11. How might we 'forget' His commandments?_____

_____
_____
_____
_____

12. What might try to come into our lives and compete for the place of His voice and words?___

_____

_____

_____

13. Contemplate the roads of the Lord versus other roads you might have taken in your life. What sort of experiences have you had on the road that the Lord has trodden for you?_____

_____

_____

14. How can we know if we are 'delighting' in God's Word?_____

_____

_____

15. What does verse 14 say about the level of rejoicing we should have concerning God's Word?_____

_____

_____

16. If you were to have ALL riches, why would that make you happy?_____

_____

_____

_____

_____

_____

_____

_____

17. How could we compare what we would do with all riches and what we can do with the Word of God?_____

_____

_____

_____

18. What sort of actions could you do to demonstrate the value the Lord would want you to put on the Word of God?_____

_____

_____

_____

_____

_____

_____

_____

Meditate

17 Deal bountifully with Your servant,

That I may live and keep Your word.

18 Open my eyes, that I may see

Wondrous things from Your law.

19 I am a stranger in the earth;

Do not hide Your commandments from me.

20 My soul breaks with longing

For Your judgments at all times.

21 You rebuke the proud — the cursed,

Who stray from Your commandments.

22 Remove from me reproach and contempt,

For I have kept Your testimonies.

23 Princes also sit and speak against me,

But Your servant meditates on Your statutes.

24 Your testimonies also are my delight

1. Looking at verse 17, what is the reason that the psalmist asks God to deal with him?_____

_____

_____

_____

2. How would the discipline and transforming work of God in our lives result in a greater place for God's Word in our lives?_____

_____

_____

_____

3. Describe a time when you were being 'dealt with' that brought out an appreciation for the Word of God._____

_____

_____

_____

_____

_____

4. How does God use His Word to deal with us?_____

_____

_____

_____

_____

5. Why is it important to pray and ask God for His help in seeing wondrous things in His Word?_____

_____

_____

_____

_____

6. If we need help seeing the wondrous things in God's law, what does this tell us about scriptures we might think we fully know?_____

_____

_____

_____

_____

7. Look at Hebrews 11:13 and verse 19. What do we learn about our identities and homeland in these verses?_____

_____

_____

8. Why is it so important for us to know God's Word while we are here on this earth?_____

_____

_____

_____

_____

9. How often does the psalmist say his heart breaks with longing for God's judgments? (vs. 20)_____

_____

10. What does this reveal about the place God would want our inner man to be in regarding our desire to see and understand the Lord's declarations on matters?_____

_____

_____

_____

_____

11. How does the Lord describe those who 'stray' from God's commands?_____

_____

_____

12. When we guard God's Word as worthy to be obeyed and heeded to, what could we trust God to remove from our lives?_____

_____

_____

13. What should we set our minds on when others are speaking evil about us?_____

_____

_____

_____

14. When people talk about us whose words do we often start to meditate on? _____

_____

_____

15. Why do you think this is the natural response to such experiences?_____

_____

_____

_____

16. What kind of fruit could this produce in our lives?_

_____

_____

_____

_____

_____

17. In verse 24 we learn that we are not only to delight ourselves in the Word of God but it is supposed to be something for us. What is this?___

_____

_____

_____

_____

_____

_____

18. How might the Word of God be used in this way? How has the Word worked this way in your life?_____

_____

_____

_____

_____

_____

_____

_____

_____

_____

_____

Cling

Ps 119:25-32

25 My soul clings to the dust;

Revive me according to Your word.

26 I have declared my ways, and You answered me;

Teach me Your statutes.

27 Make me understand the way of Your precepts;

So shall I meditate on Your wonderful works.

28 My soul melts from heaviness;

Strengthen me according to Your word.

29 Remove from me the way of lying,

And grant me Your law graciously.

30 I have chosen the way of truth;

Your judgments I have laid before me.

31 I cling to Your testimonies;

O Lord, do not put me to shame!

32 I will run the course of Your commandments,

For You shall enlarge my heart.

1. Reread verse 25. What do you think is going on with the psalmist in this verse?

_____

_____

_____

2. Describe a time in your life that you felt down low in the dust.

_____

_____

_____

_____

3. What did you do about it?

_____

_____

_____

4. In this section of scripture, what words show us that the psalmist turns upward rather than inward?

_____

_____

_____

5. What does verse 26 tell us about what the psalmist did in response to his circumstances?

_____

_____

_____

_____

_____

6. How does God respond to him as a result of his actions?

_____

_____

_____

7. Read John 1:1:9. How does this verse relate to Psalm 119:26?

_____

_____

_____

_____

_____

8. What does it mean to meditate on God's wonderful deeds (27)?

_____

_____

_____

9. What specifically comes to your mind when you think of the wondrous works of God?

_____

_____

_____

_____

10. What does the psalmist say about being dependent on God?

_____

_____

_____

_____

_____

11. In what ways are you dependent on God?

_____

_____

_____

12. Where do you find yourself acting independently from God?

_____

_____

_____

13. How quick/often do you admit you are wrong?

_____

_____

14. In verse 26, the psalmist says, *"I gave an account of my ways and you answered me; teach you decrees."* (NIV) and then in verse 29 he says, *"Keep me from deceitful ways; be gracious to me and teach me your law."* Do you find it difficult to open your heart to the Father and confess your wrongful thoughts and actions? Why or why not?

_____

_____

_____

_____

_____

_____

_____

15. Summarize the overall message as it speaks to you in verses 25-32?

_____

_____

_____

_____

_____

_____

_____

16. How can you intentionally put into action the truths of this section of scripture?_____

_____

_____

_____

_____

_____

Liberty

Ps 119:33-48

33 Teach me, O Lord, the way of Your statutes,

And I shall keep it to the end.

34 Give me understanding,

and I shall keep Your law;

Indeed, I shall observe it with my whole heart.

35 Make me walk in the

path of Your commandments,

For I delight in it.

36 Incline my heart to Your testimonies,

And not to covetousness.

37 Turn away my eyes from

looking at worthless things,

And revive me in Your way.

38 Establish Your word to Your servant,

Who is devoted to fearing You.

39 Turn away my reproach which I dread,

For Your judgments are good.

40 Behold, I long for Your precepts;

Revive me in Your righteousness.

41 Let Your mercies come also to me, O Lord —

Your salvation according to Your word.

42 So shall I have an answer

for him who reproaches me,

For I trust in Your word.

43 And take not the word of truth

utterly out of my mouth,

For I have hoped in Your ordinances.

44 So shall I keep Your law continually,

Forever and ever.

45 And I will walk at liberty,

For I seek Your precepts.

46 I will speak of Your testimonies also before kings,

And will not be ashamed.

47 And I will delight myself in Your commandments,

Which I love.

48 My hands also

I will lift up to Your commandments,

Which I love, And I will meditate on Your statutes.

17. Look at Psalm 85:11 and compare it with verse 33._____
_____

18. What does the psalmist say he will do according to verse 33 if he is instructed?_____
_____

19. What do we learn about the goal of being taught God's Word in this verse?_____
_____

20. What does the psalmist say will help him observe God's Word with his whole heart according to verse 34?_____
_____
_____

21. What is a good remedy for us if we find ourselves discontent and coveting according to verses 36 and 37?_____
_____
_____
_____

22. Why do you suppose this is true?_____
_____
_____

23. What should our attitude be towards the Word of God according to these verses:
a. Verse 35b _____
_____

b. Verse 40a_____
_____

c. Verse 42b_____
_____

d. Verse 46b_____

_____

e. Verse 48b_____

_____

24. What does verse 35 tell us about God's Word and the course/path of our lives?_____

_____

_____

25. What does the Lord tell us the Word can help us with in verse 42?_____

_____

_____

26. The Word often contains some limits and boundaries. Why do you think verse 45 says that we can walk at liberty while we are seeking His boundaries?_____

_____

_____

_____

_____

_____

_____

27. How can we practically 'delight' ourselves in God's Word?_____

_____

_____

_____

_____

28. If God's Word starts to become some sort of drudgery or duty what might be the problem and/or how can we remedy this?_____

_____

_____

_____

_____

_____

29. How long should we have such a great respect and adherence for God's Word according to verse 44?_____

_____

_____

_____

_____

_____

Comfort

Ps 119:49-64

49 Remember the word to Your servant,

Upon which You have caused me to hope.

50 This is my comfort in my affliction,

For Your word has given me life.

51 The proud have me in great derision,

Yet I do not turn aside from Your law.

52 I remembered Your judgments of old, O Lord,

And have comforted myself.

53 Indignation has taken hold of me

Because of the wicked, who forsake Your law.

54 Your statutes have been my songs

In the house of my pilgrimage.

55 I remember Your name in the night, O Lord,

And I keep Your law.

56 This has become mine,

Because I kept Your precepts.

57 You are my portion, O Lord;

I have said that I would keep Your words.

58 I entreated Your favor with my whole heart;

Be merciful to me according to Your word.

59 I thought about my ways,

And turned my feet to Your testimonies.

60 I made haste, and did not delay

To keep Your commandments.

61 The cords of the wicked have bound me,

But I have not forgotten Your law.

62 At midnight I will rise to give thanks to You,

Because of Your righteous judgments.

63 I am a companion of all who fear You,

And of those who keep Your precepts.

64 The earth, O Lord, is full of Your mercy;

Teach me Your statutes.

1. What does the psalmist say the Word has helped him to do in verse 49?_____

_____

2. What does verse 50 tell us the Word can do for us when we are going through affliction?_____

_____

3. What scripture has been helpful to you during a painful time in your life or what one would you recommend to someone in affliction?_____

_____

_____

4. When verse 50 says that the Word gives life how might affliction cause us to feel like we are being drained of life?_____

_____

_____

5. When the writer of Psalm 119 realizes he has arrogant people creating problems for him, what does he make sure he doesn't do according to verse 5?_____

_____

_____

_____

6. How might we be sure to not do this when facing problem people in our lives?_____

_____

_____

_____

7. When people cause problems in our lives what types of words seem to compete with hearing, trusting and focusing on God's words?_____

_____

_____

_____

_____

8. What did the psalmist do in verse 52 and what result did it have in his life?_____

_____

_____

_____

_____

9. Why would a person need to be able to do this in their lives?_____

_____

_____

_____

10. How might knowing God's judgments on matters bring comfort into our lives?_____

_____

_____

_____

_____

_____

11. What took hold of psalmist according to verse
    53?_____

    _____

    _____

    _____

12. Why did he have this strong reaction?_____

    _____

    _____

    _____

13. Describe a situation in which seeing a person go
    against what the Lord says would possibly or has
    possibly brought about a strong internal reaction
    within you? _____

    _____

    _____

    _____

    _____

    _____

14. What would be a constructive way to express
    such a reaction? What would be a destructive
    way?_____

    _____

    _____

    _____

    _____

15. What do we learn about singing to the Lord in verse 54?_____

_____

16. What has become that which belongs to him according to verse 56?_____

_____

_____

_____

17. What would help us turn our feet in the direction of the Lord's commands according to verse 59?__

_____

_____

_____

18. What does verse 63 help us know about choosing our closest friends?_____

_____

_____

_____

Affliction

Ps 119:65-80

65 You have dealt well with Your servant,

O Lord, according to Your word.

66 Teach me good judgment and knowledge,

For I believe Your commandments.

67 Before I was afflicted I went astray,

But now I keep Your word.

68 You are good, and do good;

Teach me Your statutes.

69 The proud have forged a lie against me,

But I will keep Your precepts with my whole heart.

70 Their heart is as fat as grease,

But I delight in Your law.

71 It is good for me that I have been afflicted,

That I may learn Your statutes.

72 The law of Your mouth is better to me

Than thousands of coins of gold and silver.

73 Your hands have made me and fashioned me;

Give me understanding,

that I may learn Your commandments.

74 Those who fear You will be glad

when they see me,

Because I have hoped in Your word.

75 I know, O Lord, that Your judgments are right,

And that in faithfulness You have afflicted me.

76 Let, I pray, Your merciful kindness be for my

comfort, According to Your word to Your servant.

77 Let Your tender mercies come to me,

that I may live; For Your law is my delight.

78 Let the proud be ashamed,

For they treated me wrongfully with falsehood;

But I will meditate on Your precepts.

79 Let those who fear You turn to me,

Those who know Your testimonies.

80 Let my heart be blameless

regarding Your statutes,

That I may not be ashamed.

1. What sort of criteria does the Lord use in evaluating our lives according to verse 65?_____

   _____

   _____

   _____

2. What part do could believing God's Word play in learning good judgment and knowledge from His Word? (v. 66)_____

   _____

   _____

   _____

   _____

   _____

3. What does Hebrews 4:2 say about the relationship between faith and God's Word having a great effect on us?_____

   _____

   _____

   _____

   _____

   _____

4. What does verse 67 tell us about what hard times can do to our relationship with the Word?_____

   _____

   _____

   _____

   _____

   _____

5. Have you ever had this experience? Explain.____

_____

_____

_____

_____

_____

6. What does verse 68 tell us about God?_____

_____

_____

_____

7. What should we focus on when other people lie about us? (v. 69-70)_____

_____

_____

8. Why do you think this is a good remedy for our hearts when we have people accusing or lying about us?_____

_____

_____

_____

9. What is one of the things the Lord wants to happen to us from affliction?_____

_____

_____

_____

10. How can verse 72 help us make it through some pretty difficult times?_____

_____

_____

_____

_____

_____

_____

11. What can thousands of gold and silver do for us?_

_____

_____

_____

_____

_____

_____

12. How might God's Word benefit us more than thousands of gold and silver?_____

_____

_____

_____

_____

_____

_____

_____

_____

13. Why can we be confident that God will give us understanding from His Word according to verse 73?_____

_____

_____

_____

14. What kind of people will want to be around us if we are a person who hopes in the Word of God? (v. 74)_____

_____

_____

15. How might having these people around us protect us and bless our lives?_____

_____

_____

_____

16. What does this tell us about our ability to attract the people that are good for us in our lives and what we can do to avoid people who may lead us astray?_____

_____

_____

_____

Hope

Ps 119:81-96

81 My soul faints for Your salvation,

But I hope in Your word.

82 My eyes fail from searching Your word,

Saying, "When will You comfort me?"

83 For I have become like a wineskin in smoke,

Yet I do not forget Your statutes.

84 How many are the days of Your servant?

When will You execute judgment

on those who persecute me?

85 The proud have dug pits for me,

Which is not according to Your law.

86 All Your commandments are faithful;

They persecute me wrongfully;

Help me!

87 They almost made an end of me on earth,

But I did not forsake Your precepts.

88 Revive me according to Your lovingkindness,

So that I may keep the testimony of Your mouth.

89 Forever, O Lord,

Your word is settled in heaven.

90 Your faithfulness endures to all generations;

You established the earth, and it abides.

91 They continue this day

according to Your ordinances,

For all are Your servants.

92 Unless Your law had been my delight,

I would then have perished in my affliction.

93 I will never forget Your precepts,

For by them You have given me life.

94 I am Yours, save me;

For I have sought Your precepts.

95 The wicked wait for me to destroy me,

But I will consider Your testimonies.

96 I have seen the consummation of all perfection,

But Your commandment is exceedingly broad.

1. Verse 81 lets us know that sometimes we grow weary waiting for an answer to prayer. What is the remedy at times of weariness?_____

_____

_____

_____

_____

_____

_____

2. How does the psalmist describe what he was feeling in verses 81-87?_____

_____

_____

_____

_____

_____

_____

_____

_____

_____

_____

_____

3. How many commandments are we to consider true and faithful according to verse 86?_____

_____

_____

4. When we are not SEEING God's Word being fulfilled in the timing we desire why might this truth be crucial for our stability?_____

_____

_____

_____

_____

5. Describe how we are to respond to such weary and dry times in these verses?
a. Verse 82 _____

_____

b. Verse 83_____

_____

c. Verse 87_____

_____

d. Verse 92_____

_____

e. Verse 94_____

_____

f. Verse 95_____

_____

6. What experience with the Word of God can really help us remember and treasure God's Word? (v. 93)_____

_____

_____

_____

_____

7. What is one of the reasons we should seek God for revival according to verse 88?_____

_____

_____

_____

8. What do we learn about God's Word in verse 89?

_____

_____

_____

9. How does this help us look at God's standards in light of cultural trends and changes?_____

_____

_____

_____

10. When you sense evil people planning something against you what does verse 95 say you should do?_____

_____

_____

_____

Light

Ps 119:97-112

97 Oh, how I love Your law!

It is my meditation all the day.

98 You, through Your commandments,

make me wiser than my enemies;

For they are ever with me.

99 I have more understanding than all my teachers,

For Your testimonies are my meditation.

100 I understand more than the ancients,

Because I keep Your precepts.

101 I have restrained my feet from every evil way,

That I may keep Your word.

102 I have not departed from Your judgments,

For You Yourself have taught me.

103 How sweet are Your words to my taste,

Sweeter than honey to my mouth!

104 Through Your precepts I get understanding;

Therefore I hate every false way.

105 Your word is a lamp to my feet

And a light to my path.

106 I have sworn and confirmed

That I will keep Your righteous judgments.

107 I am afflicted very much;

Revive me, O Lord, according to Your word.

108 Accept, I pray,

the freewill offerings of my mouth, O Lord,

And teach me Your judgments.

109 My life is continually in my hand,

Yet I do not forget Your law.

110 The wicked have laid a snare for me,

Yet I have not strayed from Your precepts.

111 Your testimonies I have taken

as a heritage forever,

For they are the rejoicing of my heart.

112 I have inclined my heart to perform Your statutes

Forever, to the very end.

1. What is one way that shows how much we love God's Word according to verse 97?_____

     _____

     _____

     _____

2. How can we gain the cutting edge over our enemies according to verse 98?_____

     _____

     _____

3. In verses 99 and 100 we are told how we might excel in wisdom and insight than even teachers or those who have lived many years. Explain.____

     _____

     _____

     _____

     _____

4. What sort of actions might we need to take according to verse 101 that would contribute to our ability to see our lives take on the quality of a Word-directed life?_____

     _____

     _____

     _____

5. Who teaches us the Word and all it means and can do in our lives according to verse 103?_____

     _____

     _____

     _____

6. How does He do this?_____

_____

_____

_____

_____

_____

7. What does verse 103 tell us about how our
   relationship should be with His Word?_____

_____

_____

_____

_____

8. What can give us a recognition and hatred for
   'false' paths in our lives? (v. 104)_____

_____

_____

_____

_____

9. What does God reveal to us about our journey,
   our steps and paths we need to take? (v. 105)___

_____

_____

_____

_____

_____

_____

10. According to verse 107, what do we need when we find ourselves in MUCH affliction? Why and how can this help?_____

_____

_____

_____

_____

_____

_____

_____

11. What do you think the psalmist is referring to as offerings in verse 108?_____

_____

_____

_____

_____

_____

12. What sort of things can come in and really try to cause the Word of God to NOT be on our mind, in our meditation or in front of our eyes?_____

_____

_____

_____

_____

_____

_____

13. How might this accomplish our adversary's plan for our days?_____

_____

_____

_____

14. How should we direct ourselves in our relationship with the Word according to verse 111?_____

_____

_____

_____

_____

_____

_____

15. In order to maintain a lifetime commitment to God's Word, how could we pace ourselves or place ourselves in a disciplined life to assure a 'forever' commitment? (v. 112)_____

_____

_____

_____

_____

_____

_____

_____

_____

Understanding

113 I hate the double-minded,

But I love Your law.

114 You are my hiding place and my shield;

I hope in Your word.

115 Depart from me, you evildoers,

For I will keep the commandments of my God!

116 Uphold me according to Your word,

that I may live;

And do not let me be ashamed of my hope.

117 Hold me up, and I shall be safe,

And I shall observe Your statutes continually.

118 You reject all those

who stray from Your statutes,

For their deceit is falsehood.

119 You put away all the wicked

of the earth like dross;

Therefore I love Your testimonies.

120 My flesh trembles for fear of You,

And I am afraid of Your judgments.

121 I have done justice and righteousness;

Do not leave me to my oppressors.

122 Be surety for Your servant for good;

Do not let the proud oppress me.

123 My eyes fail from seeking Your salvation

And Your righteous word.

124 Deal with Your servant

according to Your mercy,

And teach me Your statutes.

125 I am Your servant;

Give me understanding,

That I may know Your testimonies.

126 It is time for You to act, O Lord,

For they have regarded Your law as void.

127 Therefore I love Your commandments

More than gold, yes, than fine gold!

128 Therefore all Your precepts

concerning all things I consider to be right;

I hate every false way.

1. How would staying in and true to the Word of God protect us from being double-minded? (v. 113)_____

_____

_____

_____

2. What do you experience when you find yourself torn by two competing allegiances?_____

_____

_____

_____

_____

3. How can the Word be a 'shield' for us? (v. 114)___

_____

_____

_____

4. How can the Word be a hiding place for us? (v. 114)_____

_____

_____

5. How can having the wrong friends contribute to being drawn away from ordering our lives according to God's Word? (v. 115)_____

_____

_____

_____

_____

6. What sort of support can the Word of God give us when we face instability? (v. 116)_____

_____

_____

_____

_____

_____

7. Describe a time when the Word of God helped you feel safe. (v. 117)_____

_____

_____

_____

_____

_____

8. What is the difference between 'straying' from His commandments and 'departing' from them? (v. 118)_____

_____

_____

_____

_____

_____

_____

_____

9. What would you consider symptoms in your own life that you were beginning to stray from God's Word?_____

_____

_____

_____

_____

_____

10. What kind of energy and focus do you see in verse 123?_____

_____

_____

11. How should we see ourselves in relationship to the Lord? (v. 125)_____

_____

12. How would taking this role help us better desire to understand His Word and learn His heart through His statutes?_____

_____

_____

_____

_____

13. Why would a person sense an urgency for God to involve Himself in a situation according to verse 126?_____

_____

_____

_____

_____

_____

14. What kind of value does the Word of God have according to verse 127?_____

_____

_____

_____

_____

15. What areas can we consider God's Word to be right about? (v. 128)_____

_____

_____

_____

_____

_____

_____

_____

_____

Pure

Ps 119:129-144

129 Your testimonies are wonderful;

Therefore my soul keeps them.

130 The entrance of Your words gives light;

It gives understanding to the simple.

131 I opened my mouth and panted,

For I longed for Your commandments.

132 Look upon me and be merciful to me,

As Your custom is toward

those who love Your name.

133 Direct my steps by Your word,

And let no iniquity have dominion over me.

134 Redeem me from the oppression of man,

That I may keep Your precepts.

135 Make Your face shine upon Your servant,

And teach me Your statutes.

136 Rivers of water run down from my eyes,

Because men do not keep Your law.

137 Righteous are You, O Lord,

And upright are Your judgments.

138 Your testimonies, which You have commanded,

Are righteous and very faithful.

139 My zeal has consumed me,

Because my enemies have forgotten Your words.

140 Your word is very pure;

Therefore Your servant loves it.

141 I am small and despised,

Yet I do not forget Your precepts.

142 Your righteousness

is an everlasting righteousness,

And Your law is truth.

143 Trouble and anguish have overtaken me,

Yet Your commandments are my delights.

144 The righteousness of Your

testimonies is everlasting;

Give me understanding, and I shall live.

1. What reason does the psalmist give in verse 129 to explain why he treasures and obeys the Word of God?_____

_____

2. What two things does verse 130 say the Word of God gives to us?_____

_____

_____

3. Have you ever had a dark or confusing time and God used His Word to help you through it? Explain._____

_____

_____

_____

4. What does verse 131 say about the kind of desire we should have for His Word?_____

5. What is God's custom toward those who love His name? (v. 132)_____

_____

_____

6. What should help us with EVERY step in our lives? (v. 133)?_____

_____

_____

7. What do we learn from verse 133 about how the Lord will direct our lives? How does he do this?___

_____

_____

_____

_____

_____

8. What should be one of the reasons we should want to be delivered from oppressing relationships? (v. 134)_____

_____

_____

_____

9. How could experiencing oppressing relationships hinder our ability to do this?_____

_____

_____

_____

_____

_____

10. How does the Lord demonstrate that He is making His face to shine on someone? (v. 135)___

_____

_____

_____

_____

_____

11. What sort of emotional response might come from someone who REALLY loves the Word and sees that people are disregarding the things that God says? (v. 136)_____

_____
_____
_____
_____
_____

12. Why do you think someone might respond this way in the face of observing people disregarding God's law?_____

_____
_____
_____
_____
_____

13. What words describe the Word of God in verses 137 – 144?   _____

_____
_____
_____
_____
_____
_____
_____
_____

Revive

Ps 119:145-161

145 I cry out with my whole heart;

Hear me, O Lord!

I will keep Your statutes.

146 I cry out to You;

Save me, and I will keep Your testimonies.

147 I rise before the dawning of the morning,

And cry for help; I hope in Your word.

148 My eyes are awake through the night watches,

That I may meditate on Your word.

149 Hear my voice

according to Your lovingkindness;

O Lord, revive me according to Your justice.

150 They draw near who follow after wickedness;

They are far from Your law.

151 You are near, O Lord,

And all Your commandments are truth.

152 Concerning Your testimonies,

I have known of old that

You have founded them forever.

153 Consider my affliction and deliver me,

For I do not forget Your law.

154 Plead my cause and redeem me;

Revive me according to Your word.

155 Salvation is far from the wicked,

For they do not seek Your statutes.

156 Great are Your tender mercies, O Lord;

Revive me according to Your judgments.

157 Many are my persecutors and my enemies,

Yet I do not turn from Your testimonies.

158 I see the treacherous, and am disgusted,

Because they do not keep Your word.

159 Consider how I love Your precepts;

Revive me, O Lord,

according to Your lovingkindness.

160 The entirety of Your word is truth,

And every one of

Your righteous judgments endures forever.

1. What does verse 145 reveal about the kind of passion we can have in our prayer time with our God?_____

_____

_____

2. What should result in our lives as a result of having God deliver us from certain situations? (v. 146)___

_____

_____

3. What do verses 147 and 148 tell us about prayer and the Word of God?_____

_____

_____

_____

_____

_____

4. What does verse 149 say about using our voice to communicate with God and not just having 'silent' prayer?_____

_____

_____

5. What do we learn about the relationship people have with the Word that are following after wickedness?_____

_____

_____

_____

6. What does verse 151 reveal about the proximity of God to us?_____

_____

7. Look at verse 152 and Luke 21:33. Record your findings here:_____

_____

_____

_____

_____

8. What should we call to mind in the midst of painful seasons of our lives and how can we do this? (v. 153)_____

_____

_____

_____

_____

_____

9. We see prayer and the Word partnering together in verse 154. What relationship do you see with prayer and the Word in your life?_____

_____

_____

_____

_____

_____

10. Why is it difficult for some people to get out of
certain situations? (v. 155)_____

_____

_____

_____

11. How could a GREAT number of problems try and
cause us to turn from God's commandments? (v.
157)_____

_____

_____

_____

_____

12. Why would someone feel disgusted when we see
someone going directly against what God says?
(v. 159)_____

_____

_____

_____

_____

13. Compare verse 160 and Psalm 117:2 and jot
down your observations._____

_____

_____

_____

_____

_____

_____

14. What is the danger of just focusing on 'some' of God's truth and not all of its entirety? (160)_____

_____

_____

_____

_____

_____

_____

Peace

Ps 119:161-168

161 Princes persecute me without a cause,

But my heart stands in awe of Your word.

162 I rejoice at Your word

As one who finds great treasure.

163 I hate and abhor lying,

But I love Your law.

164 Seven times a day I praise You,

Because of Your righteous judgments.

165 Great peace have those who love Your law,

And nothing causes them to stumble.

166 Lord, I hope for Your salvation,

And I do Your commandments.

167 My soul keeps Your testimonies,

And I love them exceedingly.

168 I keep Your precepts and Your testimonies,

For all my ways are before You.

1. When people in authority comes against us we can feel intimidated. We are instructed to be in awe of God's Words in verse 161 when this happens. Why do you think God's remedy for intimidation is being in awe of His Word?_____

   _____

   _____

   _____

   _____

   _____

   _____

   _____

2. What does verse 162 seem to insinuating in the way we should approach the Word of God in order to get things from it?_____

   _____

   _____

   _____

3. What sort of attitude will we develop towards lying as we love His law? (v. 163)_____

   _____

   _____

4. What attitude and actions does the Word of God produce in us according to verse 164?_____

   _____

   _____

   _____

5. What are we promised in verse 165 as we love His law?_____

_____

_____

6. We see the word 'do' and 'hope' in verse 166. What are to 'hope for' and what are we to 'do' in the meantime?_____

_____

_____

_____

7. How can knowing that God sees everything about us provoke in us a great dependency and love for His commandments? (v. 168)_____

_____

_____

_____

_____

_____

8. Look at Proverbs 5:21-23. What do we learn about God's familiarity of our ways and our need for instruction?_____

_____

_____

_____

Choice

Ps 119:169-176

169 Let my cry come before You, O Lord;

Give me understanding according to Your word.

170 Let my supplication come before You;

Deliver me according to Your word.

171 My lips shall utter praise,

For You teach me Your statutes.

172 My tongue shall speak of Your word,

For all Your commandments are righteousness.

173 Let Your hand become my help,

For I have chosen Your precepts.

174 I long for Your salvation, O Lord,

And Your law is my delight.

175 Let my soul live, and it shall praise You;

And let Your judgments help me.

176 I have gone astray like a lost sheep;

Seek Your servant,

For I do not forget Your commandments.

1. What is the psalmist praying for in verse 169?_____

    _____

    _____

    _____

2. What place does/can prayer take in our desire to gain understanding from the Word of God?_____

    _____

    _____

    _____

    _____

    _____

3. Prayer is often our words/heart directed to God and His Word is His words/heart to us. Why do you believe these two forms of communication are vital to a thriving and meaningful relationship with God? (v.170)_____

    _____

    _____

    _____

    _____

    _____

    _____

    _____

    _____

    _____

4. How can praise and instruction be related? (v. 171)_____

_____

_____

_____

_____

5. How could having the boldness to proclaim who God is to others and our relationship with the Word be interconnected? (v.172)_____

_____

_____

_____

_____

_____

_____

6. What does verse 173 say about our ability to choose and how we are to use this? What does it say about this choice and God's help in our lives?_____

_____

_____

_____

_____

_____

_____

_____

_____

7. What sort of emotions or inner feelings can we experience according to 174? What are these feelings directed at?_____

_____

_____

_____

_____

8. What can God's judgments do for us according to verse 175? How?_____

_____

_____

_____

_____

_____

_____

_____

_____

_____

9. Who is seeking whom according to verse 176?___

_____

_____

_____

10. Why does the psalmist pray this prayer in verse 176?_____

_____

_____

11. What does he do even though he feels he is lost?

_____

_____

_____

_____

12. How can this help in times of disorientation?_____

_____

_____

_____

_____

Additional Note Pages

_____

_____

_____

_____

_____

_____

_____

_____

_____

_____

_____

_____

_____

_____

_____

_____

_____

_____

_____

_____

_____

_____

_____

_____

_____

Scripture quotations are taken from the NKJV published by Thomas Nelson Publishers

Made in the USA
Coppell, TX
11 September 2020

37241221R00049